To

_____

from

_____

DREAMS
ARE WHISPERS FROM THE SOUL

finding Your Purpose and Passion in Life

by MARCIA WIEDER

simple truths®
THE GIFT OF INSPIRATION

www.simpletruths.com

Copyright © 2007 Simple Truths, LLC, and Marcia Wieder

Published by Simple Truths, LLC
1952 McDowell Road, Suite 205
Naperville, IL 60563-65044

Design: Rich Nickel

Photos: Ken Jenkins (www.kenjenkins.com) cover, pages 44, 78
Steve Terrill (www.terrillphoto.com): pages 14, 40, 52, 56, 60, 64, 66,
73, 77, 99, 100
Rich Nickel (www.richnickeldesign.com): pages 16, 21, 24, 27, 29, 31,
32, 35, 36, 46, 51, 69, 70, 74, 80, 84, 88, 92, 94, 96

Printed and bound in the United States of America.

www.simpletruths.com
(800) 900-3427

ISBN 978-1-60810-051-4

04 WOZ 09

Table of Contents

Introduction

I was leading a Dream Retreat in Maui when I received the phone call. The Oprah Winfrey Show was looking for a Passion Expert. Thrilled and honored, I jubilantly exclaimed, "You want me!"

The show producer responded, "We're interviewing thirty authors." A little less enthusiastically I thought to myself, you could still want me. She added, "Tell us why we should select you…and you have three minutes. After all, we have many prominent people to call."

I quickly ran through the highlights of my credentials, including appearances on PBS-TV, being a columnist for the San Francisco Chronicle, even starring in an infomercial on passion. I shared accomplishments that I was most proud of such as helping thousands of people find, create and accomplish their dreams and certifying hundreds of Dream Coaches® to lead my work. I even expressed my mission, "To educate and inspire people and companies to achieve their dreams."

I didn't fail to mention how much I respected Oprah as a visionary who impacts millions of people every day and how I saw us as kindred spirits. I told her all of this in under three minutes while my heart pounded fiercely in my chest.

She thanked me and said, "We'll get back to you."

Sometimes on our most important dreams all we can do is give them our best shot, hope for the highest good, and let go. Knowing I could use all the help available, I prayed.

Early the next morning she called back and said, "We picked you." I shrieked and replied (somewhat) calmly, "I really value feedback. Can you please tell me why you selected me as the Passion Expert?" "Yes," she said. "It was simple. You were clearly the most passionate."

This made a true believer out of me on a point I teach. Passion Sells! Most of us would rather do business (and more) with people who love what they are doing (and show it) rather than with someone who is just doing a job.

When Oprah calls, you fly. I was expected to be in Chicago the following Monday. Luckily I had come to my Dream Retreat directly from giving a keynote speech so I had one good suit packed. Otherwise I would have had to either go shopping or show up wearing a Hawaiian muumuu.

The program was about empowering people to follow their dreams. Having never been on national television, I was quite green, feeling both nervous and excited. We were one segment into the show when something compelled me to blurt out, "Oprah, what was your dream when you started your company?"

After the show her team told me, "Oprah usually asks the questions." I was embarrassed but Oprah was so lovely that I quickly got over it. I guess she didn't mind either since I have been invited back.

Oprah responded, "My dream was to create a place to have fun." This is one of the richest and most powerful women in the world and she is telling us she values having a good time. I can attest to this since before the show, we laughed together in the green room when she confessed, "I found out at an early age that people would pay me to talk and I've been talking ever since."

Back to the live show where Oprah continued, "My big dream was to create a company where people would gather, make a contribution and together we'd give back to the world." The audience went wild, hooting and hollering they literally yelled out, "You're doing it Oprah!" The cheering continued and as the energy reached a high fevered pitch, Oprah calmly turned to me and asked, "What's your dream, Marcia?"

As her microphone suddenly appeared in front of my mouth, I had this thought. Most of us don't like to share our dreams publicly or even one on one. Why? If I tell you my dream you might laugh at me or I might fail and what you will think of me? But I know this for a fact. The reason why many of us don't want to share our dreams is if you tell me your dream, I might expect you to do something about it.

Of course, if you are serious and committed to achievement, you know how powerful it is to have others support you in making your dreams come true.

If it's intimidating to share dreams one on one, picture this. Thirty-five million people…and my mother watch the Oprah show. I took a deep breath and said, "My dream is that we'll have dreams again."

She nodded as I added, "And that we'll stop thinking of them as unattainable fantasies and take the first or next step toward accomplishing them.

Oprah smiled at me as we went to a commercial break. Here's a "behind the scenes" story. She came over to me, placed her hands on my shoulders, looked deep into my eyes and said, "Marcia, you know something that I know."

All I was thinking was, "I'm having a moment with Oprah." My mind went blank and I couldn't focus on what she was saying. I shook myself out of my stupor as she continued with these powerful words. Oprah Winfrey said, "It's all about dreams. If I had to attribute my success in life to any one thing it is this. I believed in my dreams, even when no one else did."

No wonder she is where she is today. I'll add this to Oprah's wisdom. Sometimes there is no evidence that your dream is a good idea. I don't like that, but it's a fact. And sometimes there is no evidence that this is the right time to pursue your dream, especially if it's a big one.

But where are you looking for evidence? Don't look in your check-book or in the stock market or on the evening news for assurance. The only place to look to decide whether or not you believe in your dream is in your own heart.

Can you believe in something simply because it matters to you and prove that you do by taking action today?

"Marcia's right!
You have to be able to identify
what you really love
and what you really want before
you can get it."

OPRAH WINFREY

1. *Get clear about your*

DREAMS

*B*essie had been an amateur photographer for 25 years. Now at 70, she had a very clear dream.

"I want to be a world famous, professional photographer," she said and then emphasized, "The difference between an amateur and a professional is a professional gets paid."

"Fabulous," I exclaimed. ***"Is anything stopping you?"***

She paused for a long time. "I'm sure I need credentials but don't want to go back to school at my age."

I listened between the words and felt what she wasn't saying.

"Bessie, what's really in your way?" I gently asked.

"Everyone is telling me I am too old," she slumped. "They're telling me to be realistic."

Outrageous, I thought. "Nonsense," I said. "What's a step you can take to show that you are more committed to your dream than to their doubt?"

She reflected for a moment and then suddenly her eyes lit up. "I know what to do. I have an application sitting on my desk for a photo contest sponsored by Kodak. Just entering would have me prove to *myself* that I am serious about this."

She took a stunning photograph of a man playing a sousaphone with golden tones of his instrument reflecting his bright red band uniform. She proudly sent it off to the Kodak competition, now mind you, along with 500,000 other entries.

Bessie won first prize which included a check for $10,000.00. "I ran out to get business cards printed," she bragged. "After all, now I really am a professional."

Her photograph toured around the world with the Journey into Imagination exhibit.

She got the whole dream.

"Bessie, what did you learn from this? What wisdom would you share?" I asked.

She looked me square in the eyes and said, "It's never too late to make a dream come true."

Until you get to the end of your life and look back on what you did or didn't accomplish how do you know if something is realistic? Most people compromise their dreams down to what they realistically believe they can accomplish before they explore the possibilities of where their dreams might take them.

Not Bessie…and not you!

"THE TIME FOR ACTION IS NOW. IT'S NEVER TOO LATE TO DO SOMETHING."

CARL SANDBURG

*W*hen asked to do something, do you open a jam packed calendar to squeeze one more thing into an already over scheduled life? Before we can create new dreams we need to make room for them.

Is it time to give up something you have outgrown? Are you ready to quit something that is no longer true for you and that no longer nurtures or fulfills you?

When your kids need you or you are under a deadline at work, you don't always have a choice. But when offered a choice, if you are invited to do something that you don't have to do or don't want to do, consider saying, "No, thank you."

Clear away some clutter to **make room for new dreams.** As you say, "no more" to what's no longer true for you, to those activities, habits, even relationships that are not aligned with how you want to live your life, you make room to ask, "Now what?"

Now what?

With new found friends, energy and time, what would you say yes to? What would you say "more" to? What dreams would you now schedule into your life?

While helping people create or discover new dreams, two of my favorite words are, "What else?" What else would bring you more joy and fulfillment, *what else would bring you more passion and energy,* what else would have you feel aligned with your purpose?

With a little breathing space, you can add things to your life that matter to you, make you happy and are aligned with your purpose. Imagine how your life will change when some day soon, you open your calendar to find inspiring projects that progress your most heartfelt goals.

That would be a dream come true life.

"EVERY GREAT DREAM
BEGINS WITH A DREAMER.
ALWAYS REMEMBER,
YOU HAVE WITHIN YOU
THE STRENGTH, THE PATIENCE,
AND THE PASSION
TO REACH FOR THE STARS
TO CHANGE THE WORLD."

HARRIET TUBMAN

The secret inside of you

*D*o you know someone who has climbed to the top of the proverbial mountain, only to realize it was the wrong mountain? This happens more often than you can imagine. Would you like to know how to avoid this syndrome? Connect to your life's purpose and it will never occur.

Consider this. An acorn is designed to become a mighty oak tree just as you are designed to grow into the best possible you. We all have unique gifts and talents and are here to leave our mark to make the world a better and more beautiful place.

Standing in your purpose, the quality of your dreams and the quality of your life will change. How can you live more on purpose? It's simple but not always easy. Here's how.

1. *Have a spiritual practice so you can hear the deeper wisdom beyond your ego.*

2. *Know what is unique about you.*

3. *Be of service with your gifts.*

If you are wondering where to find your purpose, you don't need to look far. It resides inside of you.

Look Inside Your Heart

Thousands of years ago, when God was creating life,
he asked the angels,

"Where on Earth should I put love?
It's so precious I want to put it someplace safe."

The angels thought for awhile and one said,
"Put it in the food.
Surely the humans will find it there and cherish it."

Another angel suggested,
"Put it in the ground.
Every time they walk they will feel it."

A third offered,
"Put it in the sky. That way it will be everywhere."

Finally God said, "I know—I'll put it in their hearts.
Right there inside of them.

It will be safe there,
but it will be the last place they look."

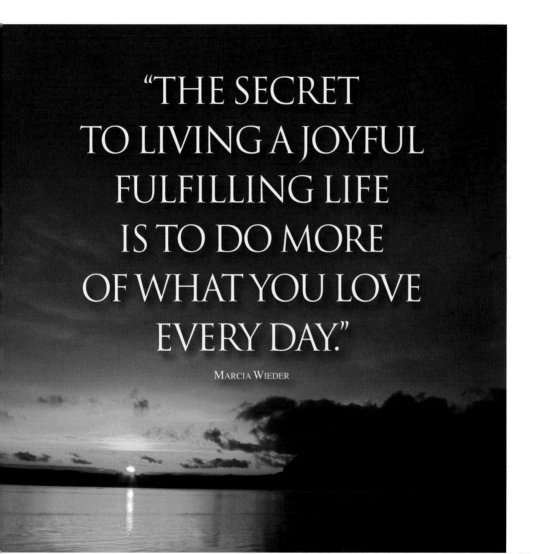

"THE SECRET
TO LIVING A JOYFUL
FULFILLING LIFE
IS TO DO MORE
OF WHAT YOU LOVE
EVERY DAY."

Marcia Wieder

*P*assion without a plan can be wasted energy but when properly used, passion can be the compelling force for catapulting your dreams forward.

Discover what you are passionate about and it will lead you to your reason for being here and to profound dreams. Spend a period of time; a weekend, a month, a year (you don't have to put the rest of your life on hold) doing what you love or what touches you.

Connect to specific memories of times when you felt joyful, and enthusiastic or even at peace. Many of us are passionate about learning or teaching, having fun, taking risks, being adventurous or inspiring, helping and loving others. ***Follow your feelings*** and look for common threads.

During the times of your life when you felt the most alive, what were you doing and who were you being? This part of you can be a powerful guide in the process of creating new dreams.

The gift of a passion quest

Make A Wish

Years ago, I hit a point where I was unwilling to continue to schedule my life into thirty minute meetings and meals. Deciding to close my marketing company in the National Press Building in Washington, DC, I vowed to find more meaningful work and set out on a Passion Quest.

Driving home one evening, I heard a radio commercial for the Make a Wish Foundation and something inside of me went "zing". Because I was on a Quest, I followed that feeling to a volunteer meeting. I remember it like it was yesterday. The room was small with an exposed light bulb hanging low over a round wooden table with paint peeling off the walls. It was non-profit land yet the work being done here was priceless.

At that table, five of us brainstormed how we were going to raise money to send a young boy to Disneyland and get another a puppy. After the meeting, I got into my car, put the key into the ignition and began to sob. I was so inspired by who these people were and the profound work they were doing, that I knew at some level this was my calling.

On that day, I dedicated my life to helping people achieve their dreams.

"UNDERSTAND YOUR PURPOSE IN LIFE BY FEELING YOUR HEART'S DESIRES."

MARCIA WIEDER

Your dream
is to have
a dream

*A*re you in need of a new dream? A critical step in getting what you want is figuring out what that is, and sometimes that's the hardest step. Many don't know what their dreams are or having been disappointed in the past, may be afraid to dream again.

Life without dreams is no life at all. When our existence gets reduced to a list of problems to solve or things to check off, passion dries up. Imagine a different list, one comprised of projects and activities that are the expression of your heart and soul. ***Reconnect to what makes you happy.*** Do you know what that is?

If someone tells me, "I don't have any dreams," I offer back, "It sounds like your dream is to have a dream." In a heart beat, they move from having a problem to solve to getting into action on something they want…a dream. It's more powerful to move toward what you want than to move away from something you want to get rid of.

Not all dreams must be huge or designed to save the world. Your dream to spend more quality time with your family or to be paid well for doing work that you love is just as important. If your dream matters to you then it is precious and worthy of pursuit.

Dreamers Live Longer

Reality is important since we need to know where we are in order to design the plan to get where we want to go. But, what has being realistic cost you? According to Dr. Mehmet Oz, author of *You, The Owner's Manual* and lead heart surgeon at New York University, it can cost your life. He says, "People with passion and dreams live seven to ten years longer than those just going through the motions."

Dr. Oz taught me a medical term called, "Apoptosis". When your brain believes you've outgrown your usefulness, which happens when people retire, get laid off, experience an empty nest, or when they have stopped dreaming, the brain sends a message to the body that it is no longer needed. The result? We begin to mentally and/or physically self-destruct.

The cure? Passion and dreams.

Connected to our dreams, we literally have a reason to live. If you think dreams are selfish, consider this. "Inspire" means to breathe, so not only is it not selfish, but it's an act of generosity, to dream. Create dreams for and with the people you love and remind them that their precious dreams matter. They'll thank you.

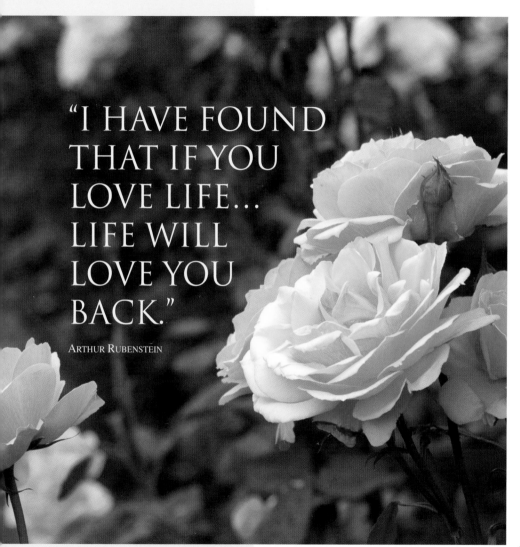

"I HAVE FOUND
THAT IF YOU
LOVE LIFE...
LIFE WILL
LOVE YOU
BACK."

ARTHUR RUBENSTEIN

A dream is simply something that you want. And where do dreams come from? You make them up. Some are based on needs such as putting healthy food on the table or sending your kids to a good school. Some of them are based on desires such as writing a book, buying a home, or traveling to an exotic location.

But by far, the most profound dreams are those that are the expression your life's mission.

Dream Insights

- You have to have a dream to have a dream come true.

- Without dreams, all you have is reality.

- Trust your intuition and follow your heart.

- Every resource you need is available to you.

- Believing in your dream is an essential component.

- There are signs showing you which way to go.
  Learn to read and act on them.

- Often there is lag time between imagining your dream
  and making it happen.

- You have the ability to make your dreams happen but
  it may require your willingness to do whatever it takes.

- On the other side of fear are great lessons.
  Stay more committed to your dream than to your doubt.

- As you complete one dream, it's time for another.
  Don't ever be afraid to cross the finish line.
  There are always more dreams available.

The Sliding Glass Door

Imagine that you're standing with your nose pressed against a glass door, so close to it that your breath is steaming up the glass. As you wipe away the steam, you see an ideal place on the other side of the glass. You see your dream.

Feel your feet standing on the floor on your side of the glass door, the other side of your dream. You're standing in the "Where I Am Now," where you live with everything that's happening in your life, including your attitudes and beliefs. Looking through the glass door, you see the beauty on the other side. Is this where you want to be?

Grasp the handle and slide the door open. A gentle, warm breeze comes wafting in and there's a delicious smell in the air. As you gaze around, you see everything on the other side that you want, everything that's in your dream, and everything you're committed to having. Your family is there, too, your friends, your dream home, your dream life. All the elements of your dream are there, right on the other side of the threshold.

Notice where you are versus where you want to be. All you need to do to get to the other side is make the choice and step across. Ask yourself, "Is this what I want? Will I commit to this?" If the answer is "Yes," lift your foot and step through.

The dream
formula

I am often asked if I can guarantee this process will make your dreams happen. In all honesty, I can not. But I can promise you this. Set clear intentions, live with integrity and in right relationship with your values, stand in your purpose and have the courage to say yes to what is true for you and no, thank you to what is not.

As you create dreams that are the expression of your purpose and prove that you believe in your dreams, I can assure you of two things:

1. You will authentically be living your life.

2. It will be transformed for the better.

This process can be used on any personal or professional dream. It has helped people double, even triple their income, and I've used it with businesses to launch marketing campaigns. One woman successfully used it to drop four dress sizes and five years later kept the weight off. With her new sense of self-confidence, she left an unhappy relationship and moved to the city of her dreams where she met the man she married. The point is, it's very powerful!

You know your ABC's.
Here are the C-B-A's for Achieving Your Dreams.

CLEARLY DEFINE YOUR DREAMS.

BELIEVE IN YOUR DREAMS.

ACT ON YOUR DREAMS.

Getting your dreams out of your head (in order to gain clarity) is critical, yet for many it's the hardest step. Remember, a dream is simply something that you want, but since our minds are filled with agendas, lists and worst of all, reasons why we don't believe we can have what we want, talking about them and writing them down is the first step toward achieving them.

Believe in your dreams by overcoming limiting beliefs. If you don't believe in your dreams no one else will either. The way to deepen your belief is to overcome obstacles including fear and doubt.

Finally, demonstrate that you really do believe by taking action. This is critical because without action, dreams are simply nice ideas. Once you are clear about what you want and believe in yourself and your dreams, strategy is the easiest part.

Read on to learn the secrets and shortcuts for accomplishing your most important dreams.

II. *Believe in your*

DREAMS

*W*hen someone shares a dream with me, my three favorite Dream Coach questions are:

1. What are you doing to move that dream forward?

2. What's stopping you or where are you stuck?

3. How I can help you?

Goldie's Biscotti

Goldie told me, "My dream is to be the Mrs. Fields of Biscotti."

"Great dream," I replied. "What are you doing to move that dream forward?

"Nothing," she responded.

"Why? What's stopping you?" I asked with genuine interest.

"I'm afraid."

"Of what?"

She turned her gaze down to the ground and admitted, "That no one will buy them."

I had tasted her delicious cookies and knew the perfect strategy to get her unstuck. I just wasn't sure she'd like it, and more importantly, that she'd go for it.

"Goldie," I smiled. "How many cafes would you be willing to take your cookies to next week to try to get orders?"

She looked at me with dismay. "I can't believe you're doing this to me," she said with a huff, folding her arms tightly across her chest.

"I'm supporting you." Staying firm, I repeated, "How many?"

"Ok," she snapped. "I'll take them to three cafes, but that's it and don't push me."

One year later, Goldie's Biscotti is sold in over fifty cafes in California and she recently met with a national distributor.

Her "hobby turned business" is already generating enough income to start a scholarship fund to send her daughter to college. With that first essential step, her business was launched.

When it comes to dreams, I don't know any other way to build self-confidence other than to make up a dream that is important to you, put it out to the world and give it all that you've got. Do we ever fail, fall short or have disappointments? Of course we do. It's called life and learning.

The true test of character is what you do in the face of a set back. Will you give up or even worse, stop dreaming all together? Or will you take stock, check in and try something new?

Coffee Shop Wisdom:
A small note on a tip jar says,

"If you fear change, leave it here."

Deal with
your doubter

There are many different aspects that live inside of us and two of them I respectfully dubbed the Dreamer and Doubter. When it comes to pursuing our dreams, The Dreamer is often gung ho while the Doubter can provide a laundry list of concerns and issues.

After a speech in Rome, a woman with a beautiful accent asked me to tell her one of my personal dreams. Assuming I'd never see her again, I decided to share a dream I had never spoken out loud, one I had kept such a good secret that even I was beginning to forget it.

"My dream is to spend the summer writing in the Greek Islands," I said all in one breath.

She handed me her card and replied, "I have a villa in Greece. Why don't you come as my guest?"

I was floored and reminded that amazing things happen when we share our dreams. I was elated, or more accurately, part of me was. Here's a peek inside my head. See if this kind of interchange sounds familiar.

Dreamer: I am so excited!

Doubter: Not me. I don't like this at all. It's far away and could be dangerous.

Dreamer: Nonsense. This is my dream handed to me on a silver platter.

Doubter/Realist (they're close cousins): Who is going to run your business while you're away?

Dreamer: My fabulous team who I completely trust.

Doubter: Well, how's it going to look to your clients that you are out of the country for three months?

Dreamer: I think as a Dream Coach, it's going to look pretty good.

When you are stuck, procrastinating or worrying, chances are your Doubter has taken over. If ignored, it can sabotage your dreams. So how do you deal with it? Turn the volume down a notch and the Doubter simply becomes the Realist, the part that wants to know the where the time and money will come from for your venture.

But before you turn down the Doubter, hear from it. It will give you valuable information such as a list of obstacles that you can manage later. Freedom comes as you appreciate its wisdom and insight rather than judging it as the enemy.

If you never deal with your doubt and you meet another Doubter on the road, their doubt will magnify yours. However, if you have worked with your own doubt, next time a Doubter challenges you, by contrast it will be the opportunity to deepen your commitment and conviction to your dream.

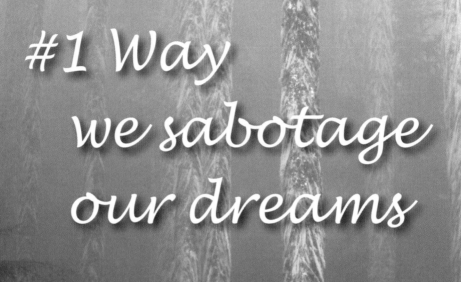

#1 Way
we sabotage
our dreams

*W*orry is the belief that things won't turn out the way we want. "But, what if," is usually the lead and favorite phrase of the Doubter.

But what if I...

...Don't really know what I'm doing.

...Go for my dream and fail.

...Run out of money.

...Disappoint others.

...Embarrass myself.

If you project your worst nightmares into your dreams, then every time you move toward your dreams you are also moving toward your fear. Here's a suggestion for avoiding this mindset. On a sheet of paper, draw a line across the middle. On the top, write your dream with great detail. On the bottom, write your current reality about this dream, including your fear and doubt.

Are you more committed to your dream or reality/doubt/fear? If your worst fears are included with your dream, you'll most likely be more committed to your reality because it feels safer. There are two reasons why people choose reality. One, if you don't have a dream, all that remains is reality. Two, when your dream is filled with doubt and fear, you'll choose the status quo over your desire.

The #1 way we sabotage our dreams is by projecting fear and doubt into our dreams.

Here are seven more ways with alternatives.

Sabotage: Negative self-talk and self-doubt are destructive.
Suggestion: Our thoughts create our reality.
Choose empowering thoughts.

Sabotage: Vagueness causes chaos and confusion.
Suggestion: Write and speak about your dream clearly.

Sabotage: "It's just a dream."
Suggestion: Make it real by designing projects with
"due dates."

Sabotage: Unrealistic deadlines lead to disappointment.
Suggestion: Create tactics, the single items "to do"
and take it a step at a time.

Sabotage: Loss of perspective can send you into a tailspin.
Suggestion: Report accurately on where you are
and what you need.

Sabotage: "I'll do it myself" thinking.
Suggestion: Get help and build Dream Circles.

Sabotage: If you kill yourself in the process, you won't live
to reap the rewards.
Suggestion: Take care of yourself so you are
available to enjoy your dream.

A new
relationship
with time

*P*robably no other complaint is voiced more often than not having enough time.

"I don't have time to pursue my dreams or to even know what my dreams are. I don't have time for me, for my family and friends. Basically, I don't have time to live my life."

Passion is the ultimate time management tool for two reasons. First, when you are doing what you love, who cares about time? When you are with someone special, or listening to a great piece of music, or painting or volunteering, doesn't time just fly by? Second, when you are doing what you love it often gets done faster.

The way we spend our time is the way we spend our lives. Can you slow down enough to get "in synch" with life, nature, and most importantly, yourself? Tune in to your rhythm and natural pulse. Take off your watch and give yourself a day off. Eat when you're hungry and sleep when you're tired so you can discover who you are, what you need and what works best for you.

Make a date with yourself, every day if possible. Even if for only a half hour, carving out time for you is a great act of generosity. *Your work can usually wait a half hour, but your soul can't.*

Whether we like it or not, the clock keeps ticking so live fully, every single second of every single day. Learn the true joy of doing less and having more as you experience each day as priceless. Fill your life with as many precious moments and experiences of joy and passion as you humanly can.

When you "catch yourself in the act" of doing something that doesn't serve you, you can choose to change it and when it's a repeating pattern, you can literally *change your life.*

One Exit Too Soon

Paula told me she recognized a pattern in her life. When she was driving on a highway, she would frequently panic, feeling like she passed by her exit. When this happened, she would get off, turn around and go miles back, only to find she had not yet reached her turnoff. She was getting off the highway one exit too soon.

Knowing that she had this tendency, she learned to continue one more exit beyond where she thought she should get off. She learned to adjust her internal clock and have more patience.

Then she asked herself, "Where else am I getting off one exit too soon or rushing through life?" Her answer was a resounding "everywhere."

63

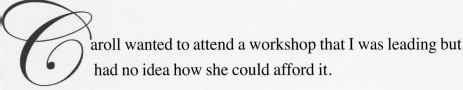

aroll wanted to attend a workshop that I was leading but had no idea how she could afford it.

"I am so sick of hearing my same old sob story," she said shaking her head. "I am unwilling to continue to let money be what stops me from having what I want. Here's my credit card for the deposit. *I will find a way to make this happen.*"

She created a Dream Board, a visual tool where she could post my flyer and her intention in plain sight. In big letters she wrote: I will easily attend Dream University®.

The next day, she opened her mail and found one of her investments was not doing well. She decided to sell it to pay off her credit card debt. She called me immediately.

"It's amazing! I paid off all my debt and have exactly enough money to fully cover both my tuition and travel expenses. This experience changed the way I look at life. I will no longer kill off my dreams just because I don't know how they will occur. I'll commit to what I want and find a way to make it happen."

Caroll now knows and teaches that it's rarely money that stops us. She has become one of my most successful Certified Dream Coaches with a thriving practice, working with exactly the clientele she wants, and on her terms. She also just tied the knot, marrying the man of her dreams. There is true power in acting on what you really want.

People often say, "I'd pursue my dream if I only had enough money." When asked, "How much do you need?" the most common answer is, "I don't know. But I know I don't have enough."

Fear and doubt can make us give up before we fully explore creative options.

Keep in mind there are countless ways to finance a dream or good idea. You can barter or trade services, ask people to invest in you, and find a myriad of other alternatives. But remember, if you don't believe in your dream, no one else will either.

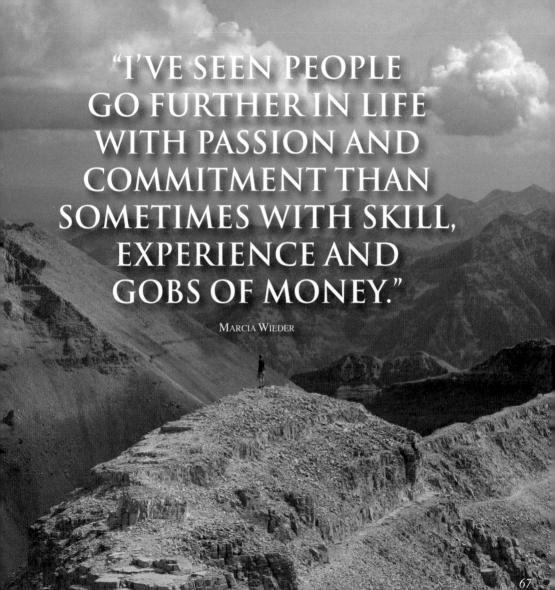

"I'VE SEEN PEOPLE GO FURTHER IN LIFE WITH PASSION AND COMMITMENT THAN SOMETIMES WITH SKILL, EXPERIENCE AND GOBS OF MONEY."

MARCIA WIEDER

*A*ll obstacles are either what I refer to as "internal," something that you believe about you, life, or your dream or "external," something that requires a plan to execute or change it. Wherever there is an obstacle, simply design a strategy to manage it. I'll go into detail on strategy in a bit. For now, let's focus on beliefs.

Our attitudes and beliefs impact our thoughts and feelings which in turn, shape our choices and decisions. Beliefs either move us forward or hold us back, but what many of us forget is that we choose what we believe.

What do you believe? Every day, actually every moment of every day, you have the opportunity to choose what you think and believe. ***You can choose to believe something that will empower and move you forward,*** or something that will limit and hold you back. On a challenging day, when you may have buckets of doubt, this becomes the critical moment to choose a belief that will support you.

Sometimes there is no evidence that this is the right time to pursue your dream. But by believing in it and acting on that belief, you make your dream possible. Moving forward on what you believe is paramount and creating a new belief is the first step in changing it.

What does it take to change a limiting belief to a positive belief? It takes willingness, courage and practice. The willingness to choose a new empowering belief, the courage to act on it to prove you really do, and the ongoing practice of doing it again and again until your reality shifts. And it will.

Grasp this concept and you'll have access to one of the most powerful tools for impacting your reality. Practice believing your powerful beliefs. Choose to believe in the power of your dreams, hopes and desires, and that you deserve to have what you want.

Anything is Possible. Dana and Steven wanted desperately to have a baby but very early on they were told that there was no chance that this could happen. The couple refused to believe this and remained vigilant about their intention. They believed it was possible. As it turned out, they were right and the doctors were wrong!

Ninety-nine percent of more than 250 family physicians surveyed from across the country said they thought a patient's beliefs aid in healing.

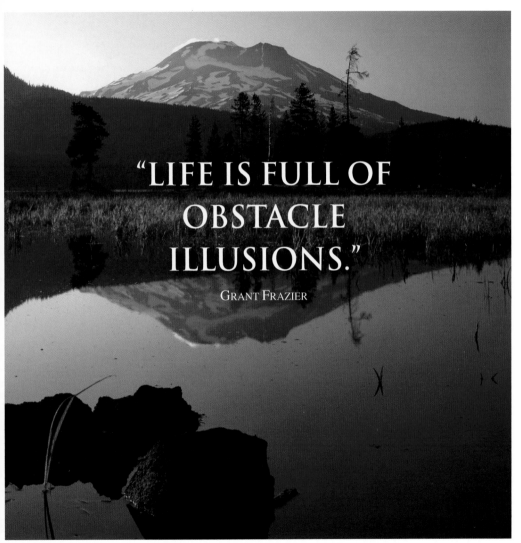

"LIFE IS FULL OF OBSTACLE ILLUSIONS."

GRANT FRAZIER

Tap
your inner
wisdom

The dictionary defines insight as the ability to see and understand clearly the inner nature of things, especially by intuition. Intuition is defined as the ability to know something without the use of reasoning. It's when you know something just because you know. There's no other logical explanation.

Having an insight is the process of having a true creative thought, right in the moment and gloriously uncolored by the past. Most thoughts are linear, come through our rational mind, and are limited. Having a flash of insight is more akin to the "a-ha" process, those ticklish bursts that seem to come from another source, inspiring and enlivening us.

I imagine you have your own means for accessing great insight, self- trust and wisdom. Maybe you close your eyes, or spend time in nature or church. Perhaps you listen to beautiful music or take morning time to journal. Certainly trust what works best for you.

Here are a few more ways.

8 Ways to Tap In

1. Believe anything is possible and look for evidence to support this belief.

2. Practice getting still to connect with the quiet place within yourself.

3. Learn to ask simple, yet profound questions that will lead you home to your heart.

4. Listen for the answers and trust that they are coming from a very wise place.

5. See with new eyes; hear with new ears and experience fresh ways of thinking.

6. Let your intuition guide you to act on what you know.

7. Feel the riches and abundance of life by recognizing everything as a gift.

8. Generously be of service to others.

"TO KEEP A LAMP
BURNING, WE HAVE
TO KEEP PUTTING
OIL IN IT."

MOTHER TERESA

III. *Act on your*

DREAMS

Integrity:
The key to
manifestation

*S*urvey big dreamers on the value they most respect and usually at the top of the list is integrity. If you are committed to living a life of joy, ease and abundance, a life filled with love, generosity and contribution, integrity is a must. All the money in the world will be worthless without it and you may even feel lonely in crowds if you are not true to yourself.

Integrity is about keeping your word and since it's difficult to create your future now when you feel encumbered, this includes cleaning up your past. How do you know if something is incomplete? It bugs you and usurps your energy. Leave no skeletons gathering cobwebs in your closets.

I have a simple and powerful process for exploring what's incomplete in your life but don't be deceived by its apparent simplicity. If undertaken fully this may be one of the most profound things you ever do. And once you clean house there is a big payoff. You will experience tremendous peace of mind with ample room for new dreams.

Here are the three simple steps:

1. *Ask yourself what's incomplete and write it down.*

2. *Ask yourself what you need to do to complete this.*

3. *Complete what's incomplete.*

Some areas where you can apply this process include: health, finance, work and relationships. When you finish, you will have a list of things you need to do. Start checking things off and do your best not to add new items.

DO YOU NEED A NEW "TO DO" LIST OR A "STOP DOING" LIST?

COMPLETION CREATES FREEDOM

Nancy was invited to re-locate to Paris but couldn't move until she sold her home. She confided that there was one room in the house that she jokingly referred to as the "black hole," since it was piled high with countless incomplete items.

Following this procedure, she listed close to one hundred "items to do," including returning borrowed books, writing overdue letters, even mailing back an inexpensive bracelet that she had taken from her neighborhood drug store when she was a teenager.

Within two weeks of completing her list, she easily sold her house and was free to follow her dream. The view from her new kitchen window includes the Eiffel Tower.

Strengthen your weak spot

While we are often aware of our shortcomings, we may not know what to do about them. If you are tired of getting stuck in that same old place, a personal practice can make your life easier and catapult you forward.

An artist I knew complained that she never had time to paint. We both saw that although she could juggle many things at once, important things rarely got completed. I offered her this practice.

"One hour each day, complete what you are doing before you move on to something else. That means, if you are checking email and the phone rings, let it roll into voice mail."

She was outraged. "This is going to stifle my creativity."

I calmly replied, "A little structure allows for more creativity."

"Alright, I'll try it for a week," she reluctantly said.

We agreed each day she would give me an update via voice mail. Here's the synopsis.

Day One: "I hate this," her curt message screeched.

Day Two: "This is the wrong practice for me."

Day Three: "I lasted thirty minutes and made some progress."

Day Four: "I am wondering why I don't make my needs a priority. I cried. I think we're on to something."

Day Five: "This is amazing. I feel lighter and got so much done."

Day Six: "I'm going to try this for another week."

Week two was so streamlined that she had time left over to organize her forgotten studio. By week three she was painting. After three months she had completed more art then she had for the entire previous year. With new found clarity, self-confidence and self-worth, her art was also selling again. Now, her assistant is managing her office allowing her to happily be where she belongs, in her studio. ***All of this came about from the simple practice of focusing one hour a day.***

Identify where you get stuck or how you sabotage your dreams. Common areas include: procrastination, over-committing, negative self-talk or not taking care of our selves. What would you like to change or develop? What could you do differently and how many times a day or a week will you do it?

Practice being the person you dream of being and soon it will become automatic and part of you. Be sure to celebrate your newly acquired skills.

"BE THE CHANGE YOU WISH TO SEE IN THE WORLD."

MAHATMA GANDHI

The
impossible
dream

I was speaking at a church near Portland, Oregon when I met Wilson. A bright-eyed 18-year-old, he confided in me that he was a Masai warrior from Kenya, Africa and this was his first time away from his tribe. I asked what he was doing in Oregon and he told me this tale.

"When I was young, I became ill and my mother took me to a medical clinic. From that day forward, my dream was to become a doctor. But it was impossible since there was no training available and no one left the tribe. It just wasn't done."

"As I grew up I shared my dream with anyone who would listen. Everyone, including my own family, told me it was a fantasy and to forget about it. But I never did. Recently, a writer came from your country to visit my tribe. He interviewed me and published my story. Perhaps you know the paper, The Washington Post?"

I smiled and nodded.

He continued, "A couple from Portland read my story and within a matter of weeks I was invited to apply for undergraduate work at the University of Oregon. A few months later, I was accepted."

I took a deep breath and said, "That's extraordinary. You must have been so happy."

His response startled me. "Actually, it was extremely painful. My family didn't have the money or any other resources to send me off to America on what they considered to be a whim. I knew there was only one thing to do. I prayed for a miracle. And Marcia," he paused. "That's what I got."

"Four families each came forward to generously extend their hearts and hands. Each agreed to house me, to feed me, to buy my books and be my family, while I was so far from home."

I swallowed hard as my eyes welled up. But what he said next rocked my world.

"After hearing you speak so passionately about dreams, I now know what I must do. I must become a doctor of course, that is my dream. Then I must return to my village as an example that no dream is impossible and the extraordinary things that happen when we gather together as a tribe."

"EXPLORE ALL
POSSIBILITIES,
CREATE EXTRAORDINARY
RELATIONSHIPS AND
MAKE EVERY
CONVERSATION
COUNT."

MARCIA WIEDER

*A*re you skilled at dreaming up big dreams but find yourself falling short in the strategy department? Or are you a great strategist who needs to wake up their dreamer? Making your dreams come true is a whole-brained process. We need to be creative and strategic, visionary and practical.

Here is a proven success strategy for accomplishing your dreams.

1. See the big picture of your dream with as much detail as possible.

2. Create short-term projects.

3. Identify the tasks within each project.

4. Assign dates to all of the steps and put them in chronological order.

5. Identify what resources can help you.

6. Make it easy for folks to say "yes."

7. Take action daily.

TRAVEL THE WORLD

One dream that many people share is to travel the world. A project I created to progress this dream for myself was to go on a free cruise to an exotic place within the next three months.

The steps to accomplish the project were clear: describe some topics that I could speak on; prepare a biography and get a list of fabulous cruise lines. The old me that used to play the "numbers game," was ready to make as many calls as it took, but the new "highly intentional" part of me took over. Wanting the best cruise I could find, I intended to get booked by the company that owned the Queen Elizabeth II, Cunard Cruise Lines.

In three weeks, I developed simple promotional materials, mailed out a package, and scheduled a date for a follow up call (to convince them this was a good idea). Before I found the cruise director's contact information, they called and booked me to go on a twelve day cruise for two, in exchange for giving three twenty minute talks on how to make your dreams come true.

While I was on board I met a lovely man who turned to be the ship's dentist. He and his wife cruised around the world, lounging by the pool in case someone lost a filling.

If we can do it, so can you.

You too have unique gifts that you can barter or trade to make amazing things happen for you and your loved ones. Money does not need to be the obstacle that stands in your way when you are creative and dream big!

"LIVE YOUR DREAM BY MAKING DELIBERATE CHOICES, NOT JUST RESPONDING TO WHATEVER LIFE THROWS YOUR WAY."

$\mathcal{B}$ig dreams get stalled, fail or even die when we put them on a to-do list. You can't put write a book or move to a new home on an action list. I once saw "have a baby," on a woman's list. When I lightly suggested there were probably a few prerequisites required, she blushed.

Accomplish big and long term dreams by breaking them down into projects that you are passionate about achieving. Remember the old proverb, How do you eat an elephant? One bite at a time. Similarly, big dreams need to be broken down into smaller projects.

Projects, like goals, have a definite end result that you will intend to reach by a certain date. I recommend you create projects that can easily be completed in one month or less. Why? We are motivated by results and a month is a long enough period of time where you can produce a substantial outcome while still keeping your passion ignited.

All projects should:

- *Be specific and measurable.*
- *Move you forward on your dream.*
- *Be easy to accomplish in one month or less.*
- *Be something you are passionate about.*

Feel what you love (passion) and what you want (dreams) and then turn them into goals and projects. But, if you move too quickly to strategy, you may compromise before you fully explore all possibilities. Act on what's important to you and demonstrate that you are committed to your dream by taking powerful steps today.

IN ONE FELL SWOOP

Aligned with your purpose, there is often overlap on your projects. This means as you check off one activity, you may progress on many dreams simultaneously. For example, I traded speaking to the guests at the Red Mountain Spa for a retreat for two. With one phone call, I moved ahead on my dreams to: live a spa life, have more fun and adventure, inspire people to dream, be healthy and fit, and travel in style and elegance, with the man I love.

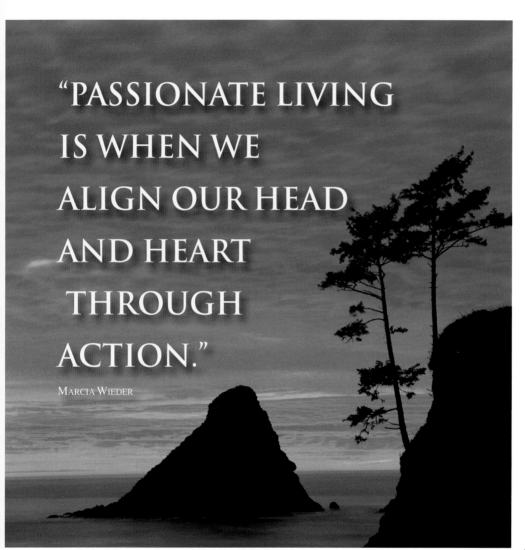

"PASSIONATE LIVING IS WHEN WE ALIGN OUR HEAD AND HEART THROUGH ACTION."

Marcia Wieder

Build your
dream circle

*S*uccessful dreamers know that great results come from assembling an extraordinary team. Share your dreams with like minded people, kindred spirits and valuable resources. A resource is everyone you know and everyone you don't know. Everyone is a potential resource for helping you accomplish your dreams.

If you can find a faster way of getting something done, do it. For example, if you don't know how to do something you can learn it or find a mentor to support you. Identify key resources and cross reference them with your dreams and projects to create potential shortcuts.

You can re-ignite passion and produce far better results when you function as a Dream Team. As you connect financial goals to a purpose and dreams, the incentive for achieving becomes more meaningful to everyone. We work for a paycheck, but it's what we'll do with the money that inspires and excites us.

People may join your team or company because they are inspired by your vision but they stay when they see they can offer their talents in a way that fulfills them. And when they are acknowledged and appreciated for their contribution, they often become life-long colleagues.

HOW TO BUILD
YOUR DREAM CIRCLE

- Identify your compelling reason/purpose
  for doing this.

- Find a powerful way to share your story.

- Be clear about where you need help
  and who can assist you.

- Don't play small. Use all your resources.

- Recognize who will be ongoing members.

- Set up a system for continual support
  and accountability.

- As your dream continues to grow,
  keep your eyes open for
  new team members.

AN INDUSTRY THAT DREAMS

The direct selling world is one arena where I often see truly extraordinary Dream Circles. Whether you refer to your team as a downline or success line, if you are part of a community where people cheer you on, or offer a much needed kick in the butt or gentle nudge, you are blessed.

The tenet for these companies is, "As you help me achieve my dreams, I in turn am helping you achieve yours." The ripple effect is endless.

In direct selling, when I hear people share their dreams, the fabulous and genuine response often is, "By when and how can I help?" It's a great way to live.

"Be highly intentional as you create extraordinary relationships and make every conversation count as you explore all possibilities."

The incredible shortcut step

While speaking at the Golden Door Spa, I decided to squeeze in a workout so I headed over to the gym and on to the treadmill. With my short legs, a twelve minute mile (on a good day) is more like walking, but nonetheless, I celebrate my effort.

I was soon joined by a tall, attractive woman, whose legs were the length of my entire body. She proceeded to do something I've never seen anyone do on a treadmill. She sprinted. I did the only self respecting thing I knew to do. I turned off my machine and cheered her on.

"You go girl," I shouted. When she was done, I tossed her a towel and we laughed. "Who are you and where did you learn to run like that?" I asked.

"My name is Marty Evans," she replied. "I'm a retired Rear Admiral for the Navy."

"What do you do now?" I queried.

"I'm the National Director for the Girl Scouts of America."

When the door of opportunity opens be prepared, even with what I respectfully call your "lingering dreams". These are your great ideas that have been hanging around for a long time, but you haven't done much or anything on them. They often start with "Someday, when I have more time and money, I'll do this."

Mine was, "Someday, I'll start an inner city Dream Camp where kids will not only experience ropes courses and cookouts, but learn the important stills for realizing their dreams."

The shortcut step is to ask for what you want and need.
Here are two tips for success:

1) Be specific and 2) make it easy for people to say yes.

If they say no, ask why. People often decline for two reasons:
1) Either you're asking for too much or 2) they don't understand what you're asking for.

"Marty, I teach people how to achieve their dreams and one of mine is to help kids." Here's the magic phrase that made it easy for her to say yes. *"Would you be willing to explore* having me do some work with the Girl Scouts?"

"Sure," she replied with a warm smile.

Now I can be found several times throughout the year sleeping in a tent. Teaching teenage girls is rich and profound and I have the privilege of doing it simply because I asked.

"ASK,
AND IT SHALL BE GIVEN YOU;
SEEK,
AND YE SHALL FIND;
KNOCK,
AND IT SHALL
BE OPENED UNTO YOU."

LUKE 11:9

Take Your Soul by the Hand

I once had a dream – it was wonderful!!!
I could do anything I please;
I could fly above the rooftops
On the whisper of a breeze.
I knew just what I wanted,
What I needed to be whole,
I had no fear of failure,
For I knew it in my soul.
But then things changed, for as I grew
My life was filled with learning –
With books and school and rule – and yet –
My heart was filled with yearning.
I searched to find the answers,
I searched to find my goal,
"Til finally it dawned on me –
I was searching for my soul.

We have a dream inside ourselves,

A gift to us at birth,

To guide us and protect us

On our journey on this earth.

We all have something special,

Each one of us' unique

You have to find the courage

To find the peace you seek.

So dream your dream and live your dream

Don't be afraid to try.

Just take your soul by the hand

And let your spirit fly.

MAUREEN WEINER

About the Author

Marcia Wieder, Founder and CEO of Dream University®, is leading a Dream Movement. With over twenty years coaching, training and speaking experience, her inspiring message, style and wit has touched audiences from 50-5000 at companies such as AT&T, IBM, and American Express. She has spoken numerous times for companies such as Avon, Mary Kay, Arbonne, Weekenders, the Direct Selling Association and the Direct Selling Women's Alliance.

Whether teaching at the Stanford Business School, speaking to executives in China, or addressing young women at Girl Scout Camp, her riveting style impacts audiences world-wide.

Marcia has appeared on Oprah, The Today Show, in her own PBS-TV special and has written several books that have been translated into numerous languages. As a past president of the National Association of Women Business Owners, she was often in the White House where she met former U.S. presidents, Ronald Reagan, Jimmy Carter and George Bush Sr. And as a columnist for The San Francisco Chronicle, she urged readers to take "The Great Dream Challenge."

Dream University events include: the Dream Coach Certification program, Inspiring Speaker Workshop, Create Your Future Now weekends and the Visionary Leader Intensive. For information, go to: *www.dreamuniversity.com*

Her free, online global community, *www.amazingdreamers.com* is dedicated to inspiring and educating people and companies to achieve their dreams.

JOIN THE #1 GLOBAL COMMUNITY
COMMITTED TO HELPING YOU ACHIEVE ANY DREAM

Amazing Dreamers is a FREE community where you can network with fellow dreamers and receive support any time, any place, on any dream.

As the world's largest and most active Dream Community, Amazing Dreamers is transforming the lives of its members. This is where big things happen and where I can support and help you get what you want, in any area of your life: relationships, career, finances, health and fitness, and much more.

Join Amazing Dreamers today and you will:

- **Access Seasoned Certified Dream Coaches** committed to help you succeed
- **Network with visionaries and experts** around the globe
- **Receive powerful Dream Tools such as e-books, films and tele-seminars**
- **Find a Dream Buddy** (great for accountability and support)

You are invited to join our community for inspiration and encouragement. It's free and available right now!

Go to **www.amazingdreamers.com**

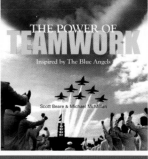
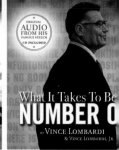

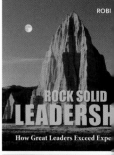